From Dent to Data: AI Innovations for Auto Body Shops

Table of Contents

Chapter 1: Introduction to AI in Auto Body Shops

- **Understanding AI Basics:** Learn the fundamental concepts of artificial intelligence, including machine learning, computer vision, and data analytics, and how they apply to the auto body industry.
- **AI's Role in the Industry:** Explore how AI is transforming auto body shops by improving efficiency, accuracy, and customer service.
- **Current AI Applications:** Review existing AI technologies currently used in auto body shops, such as diagnostic tools and automated repair systems.
- **Benefits of AI Integration:** Understand the key benefits of adopting AI, including cost savings, reduced repair times, and enhanced precision.
- **Challenges and Considerations:** Identify potential challenges in implementing AI, such as costs, training needs, and technology integration.

Chapter 2: Leveraging AI for Marketing Success

- **Targeted Advertising:** Use AI algorithms to design and execute highly targeted ad campaigns based on customer demographics, behavior, and vehicle types.
- **Campaign Optimization:** Implement AI tools to continuously analyze and optimize ad performance, ensuring higher engagement and conversion rates.
- **Personalized Marketing:** Utilize AI to personalize marketing messages and promotions based on customer history, preferences, and repair needs.
- **Market Segmentation:** Leverage AI to segment your market more effectively, allowing you to tailor marketing strategies to different customer groups.
- **ROI Analysis:** Use AI to track and analyze return on investment (ROI) for various marketing initiatives, helping you allocate budget more effectively.

Chapter 3: Social Media Automation with AI

- **Content Scheduling:** Use AI tools to schedule and manage social media posts, ensuring consistent and timely updates across all platforms.
- **Engagement Tracking:** Implement AI to monitor and analyze engagement metrics, such as likes, comments, and shares, to optimize content strategy.
- **Sentiment Analysis:** Leverage AI for sentiment analysis of social media interactions to gauge customer opinions and tailor responses accordingly.
- **Automated Responses:** Deploy AI-driven chatbots for instant responses to social media messages, enhancing customer engagement and satisfaction.
- **Content Creation:** Use AI tools to generate relevant and engaging social media content based on trending topics and user interests.

Chapter 4: Enhancing Customer Service with AI

- **AI-Powered Support Systems:** Integrate AI into your customer service systems to provide faster and more accurate responses to customer inquiries and issues.

- **Service Personalization:** Utilize AI to personalize customer service interactions, offering tailored solutions and recommendations based on customer data.
- **Predictive Service:** Leverage AI to predict customer needs and offer proactive service suggestions based on historical data and usage patterns.
- **Efficient Case Management:** Implement AI-driven case management systems to track and resolve customer service cases more efficiently.
- **Performance Metrics:** Use AI to analyze customer service performance metrics, identifying areas for improvement and optimizing service delivery.

Chapter 5: AI in Customer Relationship Management (CRM)

- **Data Integration:** Utilize AI to integrate and analyze customer data from various sources, providing a comprehensive view of each customer's history and preferences.
- **Automated Follow-Ups:** Deploy AI to automate follow-up communications with customers, ensuring timely responses and nurturing relationships.

- **Lead Scoring:** Use AI to score and prioritize leads based on their likelihood to convert, enabling more effective sales and marketing efforts.
- **Customer Segmentation:** Implement AI to segment customers based on behavior, demographics, and purchase history for targeted marketing and service strategies.
- **Personalized Offers:** Leverage AI to create personalized offers and promotions based on individual customer profiles and preferences.

Chapter 6: Optimizing Repair Estimates with AI

- **Automated Estimation Tools:** Implement AI-driven estimation tools to quickly and accurately assess repair costs based on damage analysis and historical data.
- **Cost Accuracy:** Use AI to enhance the accuracy of repair cost estimates, reducing discrepancies and improving customer trust.
- **Insurance Integration:** Integrate AI with insurance systems to streamline claims processing and approval, speeding up the repair workflow.
- **Historical Data Analysis:** Leverage AI to analyze historical data and refine cost estimation algorithms for more precise estimates.

- **Customer Communication:** Use AI to communicate estimates clearly and efficiently to customers, providing detailed breakdowns and explanations.

Chapter 7: Social Media Insights and Analytics

- **Trend Identification:** Utilize AI to identify trends and patterns in social media conversations related to your auto body shop, helping you stay ahead of market changes.
- **Competitor Analysis:** Implement AI tools to monitor competitors' social media activity and analyze their strategies for insights and opportunities.
- **Performance Metrics:** Use AI to track and analyze social media performance metrics, such as engagement rates and conversion statistics.
- **Content Effectiveness:** Leverage AI to evaluate the effectiveness of different types of social media content and adjust strategies accordingly.
- **Customer Sentiment:** Analyze customer sentiment on social media using AI to understand public perception and address potential issues proactively.

Chapter 8: AI for Customer Engagement and Retention

- **Personalized Communication:** Use AI to craft personalized communication strategies that engage customers based on their behavior and preferences.
- **Loyalty Programs:** Implement AI-driven loyalty programs that reward customers based on their interactions and purchase history, enhancing retention.
- **Engagement Analytics:** Utilize AI to analyze engagement metrics and identify factors that contribute to customer loyalty and satisfaction.
- **Proactive Outreach:** Leverage AI to automate proactive outreach efforts, such as reminders for service appointments and follow-ups on previous repairs.
- **Customer Journey Mapping:** Use AI to map customer journeys and identify touchpoints where engagement can be enhanced to boost retention rates.

Chapter 9: Automating Customer Feedback Collection

- **Feedback Requests:** Deploy AI to automatically request feedback from customers after service completion, ensuring timely and relevant input.
- **Sentiment Analysis:** Implement AI to analyze feedback sentiment, identifying positive and negative trends for actionable insights.
- **Response Analysis:** Use AI to categorize and prioritize feedback responses, addressing common issues and improving service quality.
- **Actionable Insights:** Leverage AI to generate actionable insights from feedback data, guiding improvements in customer service and shop operations.
- **Continuous Improvement:** Utilize AI-driven feedback loops to continuously monitor and refine your service offerings based on customer input.

Chapter 10: Future Directions and Innovations in AI for Auto Body Shops

- **Advancements in AI Technology:** Stay informed about the latest advancements in AI technology and their potential applications in the auto body industry.
- **AI Integration with Emerging Trends:** Explore how AI will integrate with emerging trends such as electric vehicles, autonomous driving, and smart repair technologies.

- **Continuous Learning:** Develop strategies for continuous learning and adaptation to new AI innovations, ensuring your shop remains competitive.
- **Ethical Considerations:** Address ethical considerations related to AI use, including data privacy and transparency, to maintain customer trust and compliance.
- **Strategic Planning:** Plan for future AI adoption by setting clear goals, evaluating potential technologies, and aligning them with your shop's long-term vision.

Chapter 1: Introduction to AI in Auto Body Shops

Welcome to the future of auto body repair! In this chapter, we'll dive into the world of Artificial Intelligence (AI) and explore how it's revolutionizing auto body shops. We'll break down complex concepts into easy-to-understand bits and show you how embracing AI can transform your business.

Understanding AI Basics

Let's start with the basics. AI, or Artificial Intelligence, refers to machines or software designed to perform tasks that typically require human intelligence. Think of AI as the brainpower behind the digital tools you use.

1. **Machine Learning (ML)**: Imagine teaching a dog to fetch a ball. At first, the dog doesn't know what to do, but with practice and rewards, it learns. Machine Learning is a bit like that, but for computers. It involves training a system to recognize patterns and make decisions based on data. For instance, an AI system in an auto body shop can learn from past repair data to predict issues and recommend solutions.
2. **Computer Vision**: This is a technology that allows machines to interpret and understand visual information, much like how humans use their eyes to see and recognize things. In auto body shops, computer vision can be used to

scan a car's damage and assess it more accurately than the human eye.
3. **Data Analytics**: Data Analytics is like taking a big pile of information and figuring out useful patterns or insights from it. For an auto body shop, this could mean analyzing data from past repairs to understand common issues and improve repair processes.

AI's Role in the Industry

Now, let's see how AI is changing the game for auto body shops:

1. **Improving Efficiency**: Imagine a mechanic who knows exactly what tools and parts are needed for a repair, and can even predict the time required for each job. AI can help achieve this by analyzing repair histories and recommending the best approaches. It's like having a super-smart assistant who knows everything about every car.
2. **Enhancing Accuracy**: Traditional repair methods might involve a bit of guesswork. AI removes that uncertainty. For example, AI-powered diagnostic tools can accurately identify the extent of damage, ensuring that nothing is missed. It's similar to having a high-resolution camera that captures every detail.
3. **Boosting Customer Service**: AI can also enhance the customer experience. Chatbots, for

instance, can handle inquiries, schedule appointments, and provide updates on repairs, all without human intervention. It's like having a friendly receptionist who never takes a break.

Current AI Applications

Let's take a look at some real-world applications of AI in auto body shops:

1. **Diagnostic Tools**: These AI-powered tools can analyze vehicle data to pinpoint problems. For instance, when a car comes in with engine trouble, an AI diagnostic tool can quickly identify whether it's a problem with the transmission, the sensors, or something else entirely. Think of it as a super-sleuth for car problems.
2. **Automated Repair Systems**: Imagine a robotic arm that can precisely apply paint or align parts. Automated systems like these can perform repetitive tasks with high precision, ensuring consistent quality and reducing the risk of human error. It's like having a highly skilled assistant who never makes mistakes.
3. **Virtual Estimators**: AI can also help with estimating repair costs. Using computer vision, these systems can scan the damage and provide a detailed estimate, including labor and parts costs. It's like having a virtual estimator who gives you accurate quotes without needing to physically inspect the vehicle.

Benefits of AI Integration

Integrating AI into your auto body shop comes with several benefits:

1. **Cost Savings**: While there is an initial investment, AI can lead to long-term cost savings. For example, automated systems can reduce the time and labor required for repairs, lowering operational costs. It's like investing in a high-efficiency machine that saves you money in the long run.
2. **Reduced Repair Times**: AI can speed up various processes, from diagnostics to repairs. This means faster turnaround times and the ability to handle more vehicles. Imagine reducing the time it takes to repair a car from a week to just a few days.
3. **Enhanced Precision**: With AI, you can achieve greater accuracy in repairs. Automated tools and diagnostics reduce human error and ensure that every repair is done to the highest standard. It's like having a precision tool that ensures every job is perfect.

Challenges and Considerations

While AI offers many advantages, there are also some challenges to be aware of:

1. **Costs**: Implementing AI technology can be expensive. There's the cost of purchasing the

technology, as well as the potential need for upgrades to existing equipment. It's similar to buying a high-tech tool that requires a significant upfront investment.
2. **Training Needs**: To make the most of AI, your team will need to be trained to use new systems effectively. This can involve time and effort, as well as a learning curve. Think of it as learning to use a new piece of equipment—there's a bit of a learning phase before it becomes second nature.
3. **Technology Integration**: Integrating AI with your current systems can be complex. It's important to ensure that new AI tools work seamlessly with existing processes and software. It's like trying to fit a new part into an old machine—it needs to be compatible and well-integrated.

In summary, AI is transforming the auto body repair industry by improving efficiency, accuracy, and customer service. While there are challenges in adopting this technology, the benefits—such as cost savings, reduced repair times, and enhanced precision—make it a valuable investment for modern auto body shops. As you move forward, understanding these basics will help you navigate the world of AI and leverage its power to drive your business forward.

Chapter 2: Leveraging AI for Marketing Success

In the competitive world of auto body shops, standing out from the crowd can be a real challenge. One of the most powerful tools at your disposal is Artificial Intelligence (AI). AI isn't just a buzzword; it can transform how you market your services and connect with your customers. Let's dive into how AI can make your marketing efforts more effective and efficient.

Targeted Advertising: Precision Like Never Before

Imagine you're throwing a party and you want to invite only your closest friends who share your love for classic cars. You wouldn't send invitations to just anyone, right? You'd choose your guests based on their interests and past experiences with classic cars. Similarly, AI helps you target your advertising to the people most likely to need your services.

How It Works:

AI algorithms analyze customer data—like their demographics (age, location), behavior (what websites they visit), and even their vehicle types. For example, if a customer frequently searches for information about vintage car restorations, AI can help you show them ads for your classic car repair services. It's like having a personal assistant who knows exactly who should see your ads.

Example:

Imagine you own an auto body shop that specializes in collision repair. With AI, you can design an ad campaign that targets people who have recently searched for collision repair services online or who have vehicles with a higher likelihood of needing bodywork, like SUVs or trucks. This focused approach not only saves you money but also increases the chances of attracting customers who are more likely to convert.

Campaign Optimization: Fine-Tuning for Success

Running an ad campaign is just the beginning. Optimizing it is where the magic happens. Think of AI as your campaign's personal coach, constantly analyzing and adjusting to ensure you're getting the best results.

How It Works:

AI tools continuously monitor your ad performance. They track metrics like click-through rates, engagement, and conversion rates. If an ad isn't performing well, AI can suggest changes—like adjusting the wording or targeting a different audience—to improve results. It's similar to how a GPS recalculates your route in real-time to help you reach your destination more efficiently.

Example:

Suppose you launch an ad campaign promoting a summer discount on auto detailing. AI can analyze how well the ad performs across different platforms and times of day. If it finds that your ad performs better on social media during the evenings, it can adjust the ad schedule to focus more on those times, boosting overall effectiveness.

Personalized Marketing: Making Every Customer Feel Special

Personalization is key to building strong customer relationships. AI can help you tailor your marketing messages and promotions to fit each customer's unique needs and preferences.

How It Works:

AI uses data from customer interactions and history—such as past services, preferences, and repair needs—to create personalized marketing messages. Imagine sending a tailored offer for a brake service to a customer who recently had their transmission repaired. It's like having a conversation with a friend who remembers your favorite topics and brings them up at just the right moment.

Example:

Consider a customer who regularly visits your shop for routine maintenance. With AI, you can send them personalized reminders or offers for seasonal check-ups based on their service history. If their car is due for a specific type of maintenance, AI can automatically send a targeted promotion, making the customer feel valued and increasing the likelihood they'll return for that service.

Market Segmentation: Understanding Your Customer Groups

Not all customers are the same, and treating them as if they were can lead to missed opportunities. AI helps you segment your market into distinct groups, allowing you to tailor your marketing strategies to each one.

How It Works:

AI analyzes various customer attributes and behaviors to create segments—groups of customers with similar characteristics. For example, you might have a segment of customers who own luxury cars and another who drive economy models. Each group may respond differently to marketing strategies, and AI helps you create customized approaches for each.

Example:

If you have customers who frequently bring in high-end vehicles, you can use AI to develop exclusive promotions or premium services tailored to them. Meanwhile, a different set of promotions might be better suited for customers who own more affordable cars. This targeted approach ensures that each customer group gets the most relevant offers.

ROI Analysis: Measuring and Maximizing Your Marketing Investments

Understanding the return on investment (ROI) for your marketing efforts is crucial. AI can track and analyze how well your marketing initiatives are performing, helping you make informed decisions about where to allocate your budget.

How It Works:

AI tools measure the effectiveness of your marketing campaigns by comparing the costs to the returns they generate. They provide detailed reports on which strategies are yielding the highest ROI and which ones might need adjustments. It's like having a financial advisor who helps you invest your money wisely based on real-time performance data.

Example:

If you spend money on a digital ad campaign and an email marketing campaign, AI can track how much each campaign costs and how many new customers each brings in. If the email campaign has a higher ROI, you might decide to allocate more of your budget to email marketing in the future, optimizing your marketing spend for better results.

Leveraging AI for your marketing efforts is like having a high-tech toolkit that helps you reach the right people, optimize your strategies, and understand your market better. By utilizing AI for targeted advertising, campaign optimization, personalized marketing, market segmentation, and ROI analysis, you can make your auto body shop stand out and attract more customers. It's a game-changer in the world of marketing, offering precision and efficiency that can lead to real, measurable success.

Chapter 3: Social Media Automation with AI

In today's digital world, social media isn't just a platform for chatting with friends; it's a vital part of your auto body shop's marketing strategy. However, managing social media can feel like juggling flaming torches—there's a lot to keep track of, and it's easy to get burned out. Thankfully, Artificial Intelligence (AI) can handle many of these tasks for you, making social media management easier and more effective. Let's explore how AI can automate and enhance your social media efforts.

Content Scheduling: Consistency Made Simple

Think of social media like a garden. To keep it thriving, you need to plant seeds at the right times, water them regularly, and ensure they get enough sunlight. In the social media world, "seeds" are your posts, and "sunlight" is the timing and consistency with which you share them. AI tools can act like a smart gardener, making sure your posts are planted and nurtured at the best times.

How It Works:

AI content scheduling tools help you plan and post content on social media platforms automatically. Instead of manually posting every day or week, you can set up a schedule, and the AI takes care of the rest. It can also adapt to optimal posting times based on when your audience is most active, ensuring your content reaches them when they're most likely to see it.

Example:

Imagine you want to post updates about special offers, customer testimonials, and behind-the-scenes looks at your shop. With AI, you can create a content calendar and let the AI tool handle the timing of each post. If you have a special promotion running in July, the AI can schedule posts about it throughout the month, ensuring your audience is consistently reminded about the offer.

Engagement Tracking: Measuring Success

Engaging with your audience is crucial, but how do you know if your posts are hitting the mark? Engagement tracking is like having a coach who watches your performance and gives you feedback. AI tools analyze metrics such as likes, comments, and shares to help you understand how well your content is performing.

How It Works:

AI tools can monitor how users interact with your posts, track engagement rates, and provide insights into which content resonates most with your audience. This data helps you tweak your strategy to maximize your social media impact.

Example:

Let's say you post a series of tips for winterizing vehicles. With AI tracking, you can see which tips generate the most engagement, such as likes or comments. If you notice that posts about tire maintenance get more interaction, you can focus more on similar content in the future, ensuring your posts are aligned with what your audience finds valuable.

Sentiment Analysis: Understanding Customer Opinions

Sentiment analysis is like having a translator who converts your customers' feelings into actionable insights. It helps you understand whether your audience feels positive, negative, or neutral about your brand, based on their social media interactions.

How It Works:

AI tools analyze the language and tone of comments and messages to gauge overall sentiment. If a customer leaves a comment saying, "Great service, my car looks fantastic!" the AI recognizes this as a positive sentiment. Conversely, if someone says, "Disappointed with the service, my car still has issues," it flags this as negative sentiment.

Example:

Suppose a customer posts about a recent repair job. Sentiment analysis can determine whether their feedback is positive or negative. If there's a surge in negative sentiment, you can quickly address any issues or respond to complaints, improving customer satisfaction and showing that you care about their experience.

Automated Responses: Instant Customer Interaction

Think of automated responses as a virtual receptionist who's always on duty. AI-driven chatbots can handle social media messages instantly, providing quick answers to common questions and engaging with customers around the clock.

How It Works:

AI chatbots can be programmed to respond to frequently asked questions about services, business hours, or pricing. They can also escalate more complex queries to a human team member if needed. This ensures that customers get timely responses without you having to be glued to your computer.

Example:

If a customer sends a message asking, "What are your hours of operation?" the chatbot can instantly reply with your shop's hours. If someone asks, "Do you offer collision repair?" the chatbot can provide details about the service and even direct them to a booking page. This level of responsiveness enhances customer satisfaction and frees up your time for other tasks.

Content Creation: Generating Engaging Posts

Creating engaging content can feel like trying to come up with fresh ideas on a daily basis. AI can help you brainstorm and create relevant posts based on current trends and user interests, acting as a creative assistant that keeps your social media feeds lively and engaging.

How It Works:

AI content creation tools analyze trending topics and user interests to generate content ideas or even draft posts. For instance, if there's a popular trend about electric vehicles, the AI can suggest or create posts related to that topic, keeping your content relevant and appealing.

Example:

Imagine there's a surge in interest around eco-friendly car repairs. AI tools can suggest or generate posts about how your shop is incorporating green practices or offer tips on maintaining electric vehicles. By staying current with trends, you can engage with your audience more effectively and establish your shop as a knowledgeable and relevant source.

Social media automation with AI is like having a well-oiled machine that takes care of the heavy lifting, so you can focus on running your auto body shop. From scheduling and tracking content to understanding customer sentiments and automating responses, AI streamlines your social media efforts and helps you connect with your audience more effectively. By leveraging these AI tools, you'll keep your social media presence strong, engaging, and effortlessly managed, ultimately driving more customers to your shop and enhancing your brand's reputation.

Chapter 4: Enhancing Customer Service with AI

In the world of auto body shops, exceptional customer service can set you apart from the competition. Yet, providing consistent and high-quality service can be challenging, especially as your business grows. That's where Artificial Intelligence (AI) comes in. AI can revolutionize how you handle customer service, making interactions faster, more personalized, and more effective. Let's explore how AI can enhance your customer service, making it more efficient and responsive.

AI-Powered Support Systems: Speed and Accuracy at Your Fingertips

Imagine walking into your shop and being greeted by a friendly assistant who knows exactly what you need without asking a lot of questions. AI-powered support systems can offer this kind of efficiency in your customer service operations. They provide quick and accurate responses to customer inquiries, helping to solve issues swiftly.

How It Works:

AI-powered support systems use advanced algorithms and natural language processing to understand and respond to customer queries. These systems can handle a range of tasks, from answering common questions to providing detailed information about services. They work around the clock, ensuring that customers get the help they need, even outside regular business hours.

Example:

Suppose a customer contacts you through your website's chat feature, asking about the status of their vehicle repair. An AI-powered support system can immediately pull up their repair history, check the current status, and provide a detailed update. If the system detects that the repair is running late, it can even offer an apology and provide an estimated completion time. This immediate, accurate response helps keep customers informed and satisfied.

Service Personalization: Tailoring Interactions to Individual Needs

Personalization in customer service is like having a conversation with a friend who knows exactly what you're interested in and needs. AI helps you create these personalized interactions by analyzing customer data and preferences to offer tailored solutions and recommendations.

How It Works:

AI systems gather and analyze data from customer interactions, such as past service history, vehicle types, and preferences. This information allows the AI to tailor its responses and recommendations to each customer. For instance, if a customer frequently brings in their truck for maintenance, the AI can suggest relevant services or promotions specifically for trucks.

Example:

Imagine a customer who regularly brings their luxury sedan in for detailing services. An AI system can recognize this pattern and, during their next appointment, offer a personalized discount on a premium detailing package or suggest additional services that complement their previous choices. This kind of tailored approach makes customers feel valued and understood.

Predictive Service: Anticipating Customer Needs

Predictive service is like having a crystal ball that lets you see what your customers might need before they even ask. AI uses historical data and usage patterns to anticipate customer needs and offer proactive suggestions.

How It Works:

AI systems analyze data from previous customer interactions, service history, and even vehicle usage patterns to predict future needs. For example, if a customer's vehicle has a history of certain types of repairs, AI can forecast when similar issues might arise again and offer preemptive maintenance services.

Example:

Let's say a customer's car has had frequent brake repairs in the past. AI can use this information to predict when the brakes might need attention again. Before the problem arises, the system could send a reminder or offer a discount on brake inspections. By addressing potential issues before they become problems, you enhance the customer experience and build trust.

Efficient Case Management: Streamlining Problem Resolution

Handling customer service cases efficiently is like having a well-organized filing system that ensures every issue is tracked and resolved promptly. AI-driven case management systems help you achieve this level of efficiency by automating and optimizing the case management process.

How It Works:

AI case management systems track and prioritize customer service cases based on their urgency and complexity. They can automate tasks such as assigning cases to the appropriate staff, sending follow-up messages, and updating customers on the status of their issues. This automation ensures that no case falls through the cracks and that every customer receives timely and effective service.

Example:

Suppose a customer reports an issue with their recent repair. An AI-driven case management system can categorize the issue, assign it to the right technician, and set reminders for follow-ups. It can also provide status updates to the customer automatically, keeping them informed about the progress and resolution of their case. This streamlined approach reduces the risk of errors and enhances overall customer satisfaction.

Performance Metrics: Measuring and Improving Service Quality

Understanding how well your customer service is performing is like having a scorecard that shows you where you're doing well and where you need to improve. AI can analyze customer service performance metrics to help you identify strengths and areas for improvement.

How It Works:

AI tools collect and analyze data on various performance metrics, such as response times, resolution rates, customer satisfaction scores, and more. By examining this data, AI provides insights into how effectively your team is handling customer service and highlights areas that need attention.

Example:

Let's say you want to evaluate how quickly your team responds to customer inquiries. An AI system can track response times and compare them to your goals. If the data shows that response times are longer than desired, the AI can suggest improvements, such as additional training or process changes, to help meet your performance targets.

Incorporating AI into your customer service operations can significantly enhance how you interact with and support your customers. AI-powered support systems ensure quick and accurate responses, while service personalization and predictive service make interactions more relevant and proactive. Efficient case management streamlines problem resolution, and performance metrics analysis provides valuable insights for continuous improvement. By leveraging these AI capabilities, you can elevate your customer service, create a more positive experience for your clients, and ultimately build a stronger, more loyal customer base for your auto body shop.

Chapter 5: AI in Customer Relationship Management (CRM)

In the fast-paced world of auto body shops, managing customer relationships effectively is crucial for growth and success. Customer Relationship Management (CRM) systems help you keep track of interactions with customers, but integrating AI can take your CRM to the next level. AI can help you understand your customers better, streamline your interactions, and improve your overall service. Let's explore how AI can transform your CRM and enhance your customer relationships.

Data Integration: A 360-Degree View of Your Customers

Imagine you're trying to put together a jigsaw puzzle. Each piece represents a different aspect of your customer's relationship with your shop—past services, preferences, feedback, and more. AI acts like a master puzzle solver, seamlessly integrating these pieces to give you a complete picture of each customer.

How It Works:

AI can gather and combine customer data from various sources—such as service history, social media interactions, email communications, and more—into a single, comprehensive view. This integrated data helps you understand each customer's history and preferences, allowing you to provide more personalized and effective service.

Example:

Let's say a customer has had multiple repairs at your shop, including a collision repair and regular maintenance. AI can pull together data from service records, customer feedback, and even their interactions on social media. This comprehensive view allows you to recognize patterns, such as frequent issues with a particular type of repair, and tailor your services accordingly. If you see that the customer has a high interest in luxury vehicle maintenance, you might offer them exclusive promotions or updates on high-end services.

Automated Follow-Ups: Keeping the Conversation Going

Think of automated follow-ups as having a diligent assistant who ensures that no customer inquiry or request is forgotten. AI can automatically send follow-up communications to customers, keeping them engaged and nurturing your relationship with them.

How It Works:

AI systems can be programmed to trigger follow-up messages based on customer interactions. For example, after a vehicle repair, AI can automatically send a thank-you email, ask for feedback, and provide a reminder for future maintenance. This helps maintain ongoing communication with your customers without requiring manual effort.

Example:

Imagine a customer recently had their car repaired at your shop. AI can automatically send a follow-up email thanking them for their business and asking for a review. If the system detects that the customer's vehicle is due for routine maintenance based on their service history, it can send a reminder with a special offer for the upcoming service. This proactive approach keeps your shop top-of-mind and encourages repeat business.

Lead Scoring: Prioritizing Potential Customers

Lead scoring is like having a filter that helps you identify which potential customers are most likely to bring their business to you. AI can analyze various factors to score and prioritize leads, enabling you to focus your efforts on the most promising prospects.

How It Works:

AI evaluates leads based on criteria such as their previous interactions with your shop, their vehicle type, and their expressed needs. It then assigns a score to each lead based on their likelihood to convert into a paying customer. This helps your sales and marketing teams focus their efforts on leads with the highest potential.

Example:

Suppose you've received inquiries from several potential customers. AI can analyze these leads based on their level of interest, such as whether they've requested quotes or scheduled consultations. A lead who frequently interacts with your promotions and shows high interest in your services might receive a higher score, indicating they are more likely to convert. By focusing on these high-scoring leads, you can increase your chances of closing deals and growing your business.

Customer Segmentation: Targeted Strategies for Different Groups

Customer segmentation is like dividing your customer base into smaller, more manageable groups, each with unique characteristics and needs. AI can help you segment your customers based on their behavior, demographics, and purchase history, allowing for more targeted marketing and service strategies.

How It Works:

AI analyzes customer data to identify distinct segments within your customer base. For example, it might segment customers based on factors such as the type of vehicles they drive, their service frequency, or their response to past promotions. This segmentation allows you to tailor your marketing efforts and service offerings to meet the specific needs of each group.

Example:

Let's say you have customers who frequently visit your shop for luxury vehicle maintenance and others who come in for more basic repairs. AI can segment these groups and help you develop targeted marketing campaigns. You might create exclusive offers for luxury vehicle owners, such as premium detailing services, while offering budget-friendly maintenance packages to other customers. This targeted approach increases the relevance of your marketing and enhances customer satisfaction.

Personalized Offers: Making Each Customer Feel Special

Personalized offers are like giving a gift that's tailored to each customer's unique preferences. AI helps you create and deliver offers and promotions based on individual customer profiles and preferences, making your marketing efforts more effective.

How It Works:

AI uses data from customer interactions, purchase history, and preferences to generate personalized offers. For example, if a customer regularly has their vehicle serviced during the summer, AI can create a special summer maintenance offer just for them. These personalized promotions increase the likelihood of engagement and conversion by aligning with the customer's specific needs and interests.

Example:

Imagine a customer who often brings their car in for tire services. Based on their service history, AI can generate a personalized offer for a discount on a new set of tires or a free tire rotation. This offer is tailored to their specific needs and interests, making it more appealing and increasing the chances that they'll take advantage of it.

Integrating AI into your CRM system can significantly enhance how you manage customer relationships. By utilizing AI for data integration, automated follow-ups, lead scoring, customer segmentation, and personalized offers, you can provide more effective, personalized, and timely service to your customers. AI helps you understand your customers better, prioritize your efforts, and deliver targeted solutions, ultimately leading to stronger relationships and increased business success for your auto body shop.

Chapter 6: Optimizing Repair Estimates with AI

In an auto body shop, providing accurate and timely repair estimates is crucial for maintaining customer trust and ensuring smooth operations. Traditionally, this process involves a lot of manual calculations and estimations, which can sometimes lead to discrepancies or delays. However, with the advent of Artificial Intelligence (AI), you can now streamline and enhance this process significantly. Let's explore how AI can help you optimize repair estimates, making them faster, more accurate, and more transparent.

Automated Estimation Tools: Swift and Accurate Damage Assessment

Imagine if you had a super-efficient assistant who could quickly analyze the damage to a vehicle and provide a precise cost estimate without any guesswork. AI-driven estimation tools act as that assistant, using advanced algorithms to assess repair costs based on damage analysis and historical data.

How It Works:

AI estimation tools use computer vision and machine learning to analyze photos or videos of vehicle damage. These tools compare the images with a vast database of repair scenarios and historical data to estimate the cost of repairs accurately. This process significantly speeds up the estimation and minimizes human error.

Example:

Let's say a customer brings in their car with a dented fender and a cracked bumper. Instead of manually measuring the damage and calculating the cost, you use an AI-driven tool. The tool analyzes the photos of the damage, compares them with its database, and instantly provides a detailed repair estimate. This not only saves time but also ensures that the estimate is based on accurate and up-to-date data.

Cost Accuracy: Reducing Discrepancies and Building Trust

Providing accurate repair estimates is like offering a clear map for a road trip—both are essential for avoiding surprises and ensuring a smooth journey. AI enhances the accuracy of repair cost estimates, which helps reduce discrepancies and builds customer trust.

How It Works:

AI systems refine cost estimates by analyzing historical repair data, including labor costs, parts prices, and time estimates. By continuously updating and learning from new data, AI ensures that your estimates are aligned with current market rates and repair complexities. This reduces the chances of unexpected costs and discrepancies between the estimated and actual repair costs.

Example:

Consider a scenario where a customer is getting their car's transmission repaired. An AI system that has been trained on thousands of similar cases can provide a highly accurate estimate based on current parts prices and labor rates. If the system detects a sudden spike in parts costs or changes in labor rates, it adjusts the estimate accordingly. This precision helps avoid any unpleasant surprises for your customers and strengthens their trust in your shop.

Insurance Integration: Streamlining Claims Processing

Imagine if you had a direct link between your shop and the insurance companies, making the claims process as smooth as a well-oiled machine. AI can facilitate this integration, speeding up claims processing and approval, and ultimately expediting the repair workflow.

How It Works:

AI can integrate with insurance systems to automatically submit repair estimates and track the status of claims. This integration allows for real-time communication between your shop and the insurance companies, reducing the administrative burden and speeding up approval processes.

Example:

Suppose a customer's vehicle has been involved in an accident and they're filing an insurance claim. With AI integration, the repair estimate generated by your system can be automatically sent to the insurance company. The system can also track the claim's progress and update both you and the customer on its status. This streamlines the entire process, reduces paperwork, and speeds up the repair work.

Historical Data Analysis: Refining Estimates Over Time

Using historical data to refine cost estimates is like having a weather app that gets more accurate over time as it learns from past weather patterns. AI leverages historical data to continuously improve the accuracy of repair cost estimates.

How It Works:

AI systems analyze data from previous repairs, including costs, types of damage, and repair times, to enhance the accuracy of future estimates. By learning from past experiences, AI can identify patterns and adjust its algorithms to provide more precise estimates.

Example:

If your shop frequently deals with collision repairs, the AI can analyze past collision repair data to identify trends, such as common types of damage and associated costs. If it finds that repairing certain types of damage typically requires additional labor or parts, it can adjust future estimates accordingly. Over time, this continual refinement ensures that your estimates become more accurate and reliable.

Customer Communication: Clarity and Transparency

Clear and transparent communication about repair estimates is like having a detailed menu at a restaurant—customers know exactly what they're getting and how much it will cost. AI can help communicate estimates more clearly and efficiently, providing detailed breakdowns and explanations.

How It Works:

AI tools can generate detailed estimates that include itemized lists of labor, parts, and other costs. These tools can also provide visual explanations, such as annotated images of the damage or interactive cost breakdowns. This level of detail helps customers understand exactly what they're paying for and why.

Example:

When providing a repair estimate, AI can generate a report that includes an itemized breakdown of costs—labor, parts, and any additional fees. It can also include visual aids, such as annotated photos of the damaged areas, showing how each component contributes to the overall cost. This transparency helps customers make informed decisions and reduces the likelihood of misunderstandings or disputes.

By integrating AI into your repair estimation process, you can achieve greater speed, accuracy, and clarity. Automated estimation tools streamline damage assessment and cost calculation, while AI enhances the precision of your estimates, reduces discrepancies, and integrates seamlessly with insurance systems. Historical data analysis helps refine your estimates over time, and AI-driven communication tools ensure that customers receive clear, detailed, and transparent information about their repairs. Embracing AI for optimizing repair estimates not only improves operational efficiency but also builds stronger, more trusting relationships with your customers.

Chapter 7: Social Media Insights and Analytics

Social media is a powerful tool for auto body shops, allowing you to connect with customers, promote your services, and build your brand. But to make the most of your social media presence, you need to understand what's working, what isn't, and what's on the horizon. This is where AI comes in. By leveraging AI for social media insights and analytics, you can gain a deeper understanding of trends, monitor your competitors, track performance, evaluate content, and gauge customer sentiment. Let's dive into how AI can help you master these aspects of social media.

Trend Identification: Staying Ahead of the Curve

Think of trend identification as having a radar that detects upcoming weather changes. Just as a weather radar helps you prepare for storms or sunny days, AI helps you spot emerging trends in social media conversations related to your auto body shop. This insight allows you to stay ahead of market changes and adapt your strategies accordingly.

How It Works:

AI tools analyze vast amounts of social media data to identify patterns and trends. These tools can recognize spikes in specific topics or hashtags related to your industry, track shifts in customer interests, and highlight emerging conversations that may impact your business.

Example:

Suppose there's a growing buzz about electric vehicle repairs on social media. An AI tool can detect this trend by analyzing the frequency of related keywords and hashtags. With this insight, you can proactively create content or promotions focused on electric vehicle maintenance, positioning your shop as a leader in this emerging area and attracting customers interested in these services.

Competitor Analysis: Learning from Others

Competitor analysis is like having a spyglass that lets you see what's happening with other auto body shops in your area. AI tools can monitor your competitors' social media activity, giving you insights into their strategies and helping you identify opportunities for your own business.

How It Works:

AI tools track competitors' social media posts, engagement levels, and customer interactions. By analyzing this data, you can understand their marketing strategies, see what types of content they're sharing, and gauge how their audience is responding.

Example:

If a competitor is running a successful social media campaign featuring customer testimonials, an AI tool can show you how well it's performing in terms of likes, shares, and comments. You might discover that their posts about customer experiences are generating significant engagement. Armed with this knowledge, you could consider creating similar content or refining your own strategy to better engage your audience.

Performance Metrics: Measuring Success

Tracking performance metrics is like using a fitness tracker to monitor your progress and adjust your workout routine. AI helps you track and analyze social media performance metrics such as engagement rates, reach, and conversion statistics, enabling you to measure the success of your social media efforts and make data-driven decisions.

How It Works:

AI tools collect and analyze data on various performance metrics from your social media platforms. This includes metrics like the number of likes, shares, comments, click-through rates, and conversion rates. AI then generates reports and visualizations to help you understand how your social media content is performing.

Example:

Let's say you run a social media campaign promoting a special discount on collision repairs. AI tools can track how many people engaged with the post, clicked through to your website, and ultimately redeemed the offer. By analyzing these metrics, you can determine the effectiveness of the campaign and identify areas for improvement in future promotions.

Content Effectiveness: Finding What Works

Evaluating content effectiveness is like experimenting with different recipes to find the one that your family loves the most. AI helps you assess which types of social media content—such as images, videos, or blog posts—perform best, so you can focus on creating more of what resonates with your audience.

How It Works:

AI tools analyze the performance of various content types, looking at engagement metrics such as likes, shares, comments, and click-through rates. This analysis helps you understand which content is most effective and why, allowing you to adjust your strategy to better meet your audience's preferences.

Example:

If you notice that video content showcasing behind-the-scenes looks at your repair shop generates more engagement than static images, AI can help you identify this trend. Based on these insights, you might decide to invest more in video content, such as repair process walkthroughs or staff interviews, to boost your social media performance.

Customer Sentiment: Understanding Public Perception

Analyzing customer sentiment is like having a mood ring that tells you how people feel about your business. AI helps you gauge public perception by analyzing social media conversations and feedback, allowing you to address potential issues proactively and improve your reputation.

How It Works:

AI tools use natural language processing to analyze the tone and sentiment of social media posts and comments about your shop. They can categorize sentiment as positive, negative, or neutral and identify specific issues or concerns that customers are expressing.

Example:

If AI tools detect a spike in negative sentiment related to a recent repair issue, you'll receive alerts about the potential problem. For instance, if several customers are complaining about delays in repair times, you can take immediate action to address these concerns, such as improving communication or streamlining your repair process. Conversely, positive sentiment analysis can help you identify what your customers appreciate and promote those aspects of your business.

Leveraging AI for social media insights and analytics can dramatically enhance how you manage your online presence. By utilizing AI for trend identification, competitor analysis, performance metrics, content effectiveness, and customer sentiment, you gain valuable insights that help you stay ahead of market trends, refine your strategies, and improve customer satisfaction. With these tools, you can make data-driven decisions, optimize your social media efforts, and build a stronger, more engaging online presence for your auto body shop.

Chapter 8: AI for Customer Engagement and Retention

In the competitive world of auto body shops, keeping customers engaged and ensuring they return can be as challenging as repairing a complex dent. Fortunately, AI offers powerful tools to enhance customer engagement and retention, making it easier to build lasting relationships with your clients. By harnessing AI for personalized communication, loyalty programs, engagement analytics, proactive outreach, and customer journey mapping, you can create a more connected and satisfied customer base. Let's dive into how AI can help you excel in these areas.

Personalized Communication: Crafting Messages That Resonate

Personalized communication is like having a conversation with a friend who knows exactly what you like and what you need. AI enables you to craft messages that resonate with individual customers based on their behavior and preferences, making your communication more effective and engaging.

How It Works:

AI systems analyze customer data such as service history, purchase patterns, and interaction history. This analysis allows you to segment your customers and tailor your communication to their specific interests and needs. For instance, if a customer frequently uses your shop for collision repairs, AI can help you create targeted messages about special offers on collision-related services or tips for maintaining their vehicle after a collision.

Example:

Imagine a customer who regularly brings their SUV in for maintenance. Using AI, you can analyze their service history and preferences, then send a personalized email with a special offer on a tire rotation, which is due based on their vehicle's mileage. This targeted approach makes the customer feel valued and increases the likelihood of them taking advantage of your offer.

Loyalty Programs: Rewarding Customers for Their Loyalty

Loyalty programs are like giving a gold star to a student who consistently performs well. AI-driven loyalty programs reward customers based on their interactions and purchase history, encouraging them to return to your shop and strengthening their loyalty.

How It Works:

AI can track customer interactions, purchases, and engagement levels to create a dynamic loyalty program. It can analyze data to determine which rewards or incentives are most appealing to different customer segments. For example, frequent visitors might earn points that can be redeemed for discounts or free services, while infrequent customers might receive personalized offers to encourage them to return.

Example:

Let's say you implement a loyalty program where customers earn points for every service they have done at your shop. An AI system can track these points and automatically notify customers when they're eligible for a reward. If a customer has accumulated enough points, the system might offer them a discount on their next service or a complimentary detailing. This kind of program not only rewards loyal customers but also motivates them to keep coming back.

Engagement Analytics: Understanding What Drives Loyalty

Engagement analytics is like having a dashboard that shows you which aspects of your business are driving customer satisfaction and loyalty. AI tools analyze engagement metrics to identify the factors that contribute to customer loyalty, allowing you to refine your strategies and improve customer relationships.

How It Works:

AI collects and analyzes data on various engagement metrics, such as email open rates, social media interactions, and service feedback. By examining this data, AI identifies patterns and trends that reveal what drives customer satisfaction and loyalty. For example, AI might find that customers who receive timely follow-up messages are more likely to return for future services.

Example:

Suppose you notice that customers who receive personalized service reminders are more likely to return for scheduled maintenance. AI can analyze data from these reminders and compare it to customer retention rates. If the data shows a positive correlation, you can use these insights to adjust your communication strategy, such as increasing the frequency of reminders or offering additional incentives for timely service.

Proactive Outreach: Staying Ahead of Customer Needs

Proactive outreach is like having a thoughtful friend who reminds you about important events before they happen. AI automates proactive outreach efforts, such as sending reminders for service appointments or following up on previous repairs, ensuring that you stay top-of-mind with your customers.

How It Works:

AI systems can be programmed to send automated reminders and follow-ups based on customer data and service schedules. For example, if a customer's vehicle is due for a regular maintenance check, AI can automatically send them a reminder email or text message. Similarly, after a repair, AI can follow up with a satisfaction survey or a thank-you note.

Example:

If you have a customer who recently had their car repaired, AI can automatically send a follow-up email thanking them for their business and asking for feedback on their experience. Additionally, the system might send a reminder a few months later when their vehicle is due for its next maintenance service. This proactive approach helps maintain customer engagement and encourages repeat visits.

Customer Journey Mapping: Enhancing Key Touchpoints

Customer journey mapping is like charting a course for a road trip, helping you understand the key stops along the way. AI maps out customer journeys and identifies touchpoints where engagement can be enhanced, leading to better retention rates.

How It Works:

AI analyzes the entire customer journey, from the initial contact with your shop to post-service interactions. By identifying key touchpoints—such as appointment scheduling, service completion, and follow-up—AI helps you understand where improvements can be made to enhance the customer experience.

Example:

If AI maps out a customer journey and identifies that many customers drop off after their initial service, you might find that the follow-up process is lacking. By improving follow-up communications, such as sending personalized service reminders or exclusive offers, you can address this gap and encourage customers to return for future services.

Implementing AI for customer engagement and retention can transform how you interact with and retain your clients. By leveraging AI for personalized communication, loyalty programs, engagement analytics, proactive outreach, and customer journey mapping, you can create a more engaging and satisfying experience for your customers. This not only boosts customer loyalty but also helps drive repeat business and strengthen your auto body shop's reputation. Embracing these AI-driven strategies ensures you're not just meeting customer expectations but exceeding them, fostering long-term relationships and success.

Chapter 9: Automating Customer Feedback Collection

In any business, understanding how your customers feel about your services is crucial for improving and staying competitive. Collecting and analyzing feedback helps you identify what's working well and where there's room for improvement. However, manually handling feedback collection and analysis can be time-consuming and prone to errors. Fortunately, AI offers robust tools to automate and enhance this process. In this chapter, we'll explore how AI can help you automate customer feedback collection, analyze sentiment, categorize responses, generate actionable insights, and drive continuous improvement in your auto body shop.

Feedback Requests: Ensuring Timely and Relevant Input

Automating feedback requests is like having a friendly assistant who follows up with your customers to get their thoughts, right after their visit. AI can handle this process efficiently, ensuring that you get timely and relevant feedback without adding extra work to your plate.

How It Works:

AI tools can be programmed to automatically send feedback requests to customers after their service is completed. This can be done through various channels such as email, SMS, or even automated phone calls. The system can be set up to send these requests at an optimal time, ensuring that the feedback is fresh and relevant.

Example:

Imagine a customer just had their car repaired at your shop. An AI system can automatically send a personalized email asking for their feedback on the service they received. This email could include a simple survey with a few questions about their experience. By automating this process, you ensure that every customer is asked for their feedback, which helps you gather a comprehensive set of data on your service quality.

Sentiment Analysis: Identifying Positive and Negative Trends

Sentiment analysis is like having a magnifying glass that reveals how your customers really feel about your services. AI can analyze the feedback you receive to determine whether the sentiments are positive, negative, or neutral, helping you understand broader trends and specific areas of concern.

How It Works:

AI sentiment analysis tools use natural language processing (NLP) to evaluate the tone and sentiment of feedback. These tools categorize feedback into different sentiment categories, such as happy, frustrated, or indifferent. By analyzing large volumes of feedback, AI can identify common themes and trends in customer emotions.

Example:

If many customers leave feedback praising your quick service, the AI system will identify this positive sentiment and highlight it as a strength. Conversely, if there's a recurring issue mentioned in the feedback, like long wait times, the AI will flag this as a negative trend. This allows you to focus on addressing any recurring problems and capitalize on what your customers appreciate.

Response Analysis: Categorizing and Prioritizing Feedback

Analyzing feedback responses is like sorting through a pile of mail to find important letters. AI can categorize and prioritize feedback responses based on common issues and their frequency, helping you address the most pressing concerns efficiently.

How It Works:

AI tools can analyze feedback to identify and categorize different types of responses. For example, feedback might be categorized into various themes such as "service quality," "timeliness," or "customer service." The AI can then prioritize these categories based on how frequently they appear and their impact on customer satisfaction.

Example:

If your feedback shows that several customers are complaining about the quality of repairs, AI can group these comments together and prioritize them for review. This helps you quickly identify and address issues that are affecting multiple customers, rather than reacting to individual complaints in isolation.

Actionable Insights: Guiding Service Improvements

Generating actionable insights from feedback is like having a map that shows you where improvements are needed. AI can help you understand what changes will have the most significant impact on your customer satisfaction and service quality.

How It Works:

AI analyzes the categorized feedback and identifies specific patterns and areas for improvement. For instance, if feedback indicates that customers are unhappy with the clarity of communication regarding repair updates, AI can highlight this as an area needing attention. You can then use these insights to make targeted improvements to your service.

Example:

If the AI reveals that many customers are dissatisfied with the way repair costs are communicated, you might decide to implement clearer, more detailed cost breakdowns in your estimates. This change can help improve transparency and customer satisfaction, addressing the specific concern highlighted by the feedback.

Continuous Improvement: Refining Your Services

Continuous improvement is like fine-tuning a musical instrument to keep it in perfect pitch. AI-driven feedback loops help you continuously monitor and refine your service offerings based on customer input, ensuring that you're always improving.

How It Works:

AI systems can set up feedback loops that regularly analyze new feedback data and track changes in customer sentiment over time. This ongoing analysis helps you gauge the effectiveness of any changes you've made and identify new areas for improvement.

Example:

After implementing changes based on customer feedback, you can use AI to monitor whether there's an improvement in the sentiment and satisfaction scores. If the feedback shows positive trends, it confirms that your changes are having the desired effect. If issues persist, the AI can help you identify new areas to address and keep refining your services.

Automating customer feedback collection with AI brings efficiency and depth to understanding your clients' experiences. By deploying AI to handle feedback requests, analyze sentiment, categorize responses, generate actionable insights, and drive continuous improvement, you can enhance your service quality and customer satisfaction. This approach not only saves time but also ensures that you're making informed decisions based on comprehensive, real-time data. Embracing AI for feedback collection helps your auto body shop stay responsive to customer needs, continually improve your offerings, and build stronger relationships with your clients.

Chapter 10: Future Directions and Innovations in AI for Auto Body Shops

The world of technology is ever-evolving, and artificial intelligence (AI) is no exception. As an auto body shop owner, staying ahead of technological trends can set you apart from the competition and ensure your business thrives in the future. In this chapter, we'll explore the advancements in AI technology, how AI will integrate with emerging automotive trends, the importance of continuous learning, ethical considerations, and strategic planning for future AI adoption. By understanding these aspects, you'll be better prepared to harness the power of AI for your shop's growth and success.

Advancements in AI Technology: Keeping Up with the Cutting Edge

AI technology is advancing rapidly, much like how smartphones have evolved from basic communication tools to powerful computers in our pockets. Staying informed about the latest AI advancements allows you to take advantage of new tools and capabilities that can benefit your auto body shop.

Key Advancements to Watch For:

1. **Machine Learning and Deep Learning:** These technologies enable AI systems to improve their performance over time by learning from data. In auto body shops, this means better damage assessment tools and more accurate repair estimates as AI systems get better with each interaction.
2. **Natural Language Processing (NLP):** NLP allows AI to understand and generate human language. This can enhance customer service through more sophisticated chatbots and automated communication systems that can handle complex inquiries.
3. **Computer Vision:** Computer vision technology enables AI to interpret and understand visual information. This is particularly useful for automating damage assessments and integrating with advanced diagnostic tools.

Example:

Imagine an AI tool that uses computer vision to inspect vehicle damage and provide repair estimates. As the technology advances, these tools could become more precise, accurately detecting even minor damage and offering detailed repair recommendations.

AI Integration with Emerging Trends

As the automotive industry evolves, AI will play a crucial role in integrating with emerging trends such as electric vehicles (EVs), autonomous driving, and smart repair technologies. Embracing these integrations will help your shop stay relevant and competitive.

1. Electric Vehicles (EVs):

EVs are becoming increasingly popular, and their unique components and technologies require specialized repair knowledge. AI can help by providing training resources, diagnostic tools, and repair procedures specific to EVs.

Example:

AI-powered diagnostic tools can be used to analyze battery performance and identify issues in electric vehicles. This integration ensures that your shop is equipped to handle the unique needs of EV owners and attract this growing customer segment.

2. Autonomous Driving:

Autonomous vehicles rely on complex sensor systems and software. AI can assist in diagnosing and repairing these systems, ensuring that your shop is ready for the future of driving.

Example:

If an autonomous vehicle's sensor system needs calibration or repair, AI tools can guide your technicians through the process, using data from similar vehicles to ensure accurate repairs.

3. Smart Repair Technologies:

Smart repair technologies, such as robotic systems and automated tools, are becoming more common in auto body shops. AI can enhance these technologies by improving their precision and efficiency.

Example:

Imagine a robotic system that uses AI to automate the sanding process. The AI can adjust the robot's movements in real-time based on the surface's condition, ensuring a flawless finish and reducing manual labor.

Continuous Learning: Adapting to New AI Innovations

Just as auto body repair techniques evolve, so do AI technologies. Continuous learning and adaptation are crucial to ensuring that your shop remains competitive and takes full advantage of new innovations.

Strategies for Continuous Learning:

1. **Stay Informed:** Regularly read industry publications, attend conferences, and participate in webinars to stay up-to-date with the latest AI developments.
2. **Training and Development:** Invest in training programs for your staff to familiarize them with new AI tools and technologies. This ensures that they are equipped to leverage these tools effectively.
3. **Collaborate with Experts:** Partner with technology providers and AI experts to gain insights into how new innovations can be integrated into your shop.

Example:

If a new AI-powered diagnostic tool is released, enroll your technicians in training sessions to learn how to use it effectively. This not only keeps your team skilled but also enhances your shop's capabilities.

Ethical Considerations: Ensuring Trust and Compliance

As you integrate AI into your auto body shop, it's essential to address ethical considerations related to data privacy, transparency, and customer trust. Ensuring ethical practices helps maintain a positive reputation and comply with regulations.

Key Ethical Considerations:

1. **Data Privacy:** Safeguard customer data by implementing robust security measures and ensuring compliance with data protection regulations.
2. **Transparency:** Be transparent with customers about how their data is used and how AI tools impact their service experience.
3. **Bias and Fairness:** Ensure that AI systems are designed and tested to avoid biases that could affect service quality or customer treatment.

Example:

If you use AI to analyze customer feedback, ensure that the data is anonymized and stored securely. Additionally, clearly communicate to customers how their feedback will be used to improve services and maintain trust.

Strategic Planning: Setting Goals for Future AI Adoption

Strategic planning is like mapping out a road trip; it involves setting clear goals, evaluating options, and aligning new technologies with your shop's vision. Effective planning ensures that AI adoption supports your long-term objectives.

Steps for Strategic Planning:

1. **Set Clear Goals:** Define what you want to achieve with AI adoption, such as improving service efficiency, enhancing customer experience, or expanding your service offerings.
2. **Evaluate Technologies:** Research and evaluate potential AI technologies that align with your goals. Consider factors such as cost, ease of integration, and potential benefits.
3. **Align with Vision:** Ensure that any new AI technologies align with your shop's long-term vision and business strategy. Develop a roadmap for implementation and continuous improvement.

Example:

If your goal is to enhance customer service with AI, start by evaluating chatbots and automated communication tools. Plan for gradual implementation, beginning with basic features and expanding as your team becomes more comfortable with the technology.

The future of AI in auto body shops is filled with exciting possibilities. By staying informed about advancements, integrating with emerging trends, committing to continuous learning, addressing ethical considerations, and planning strategically, you can position your shop for success in the evolving landscape of automotive repair. Embracing these future directions ensures that your shop remains competitive, innovative, and responsive to the changing needs of the industry. With AI as a partner, you'll be well-equipped to navigate the future and drive your auto body shop towards continued growth and excellence.

www.ingramcontent.com/pod-product-compliance
Lightning Source LLC
Chambersburg PA
CBHW051535240526
45471CB00020B/2684